MW00945336

101 Common Japanese Idioms
in Plain English

Clay & Yumi Boutwell

ISBN: 1463588801
ISBN-13: 978-1463588809

INTRODUCTION

Once one zooms beyond the basics of a language, idiomatic expressions, proverbs, and slang can provide the spice to keep motivation up and progress going forward. This book will introduce 101 of the most common—and useful—Japanese idioms.

We are including at no extra charge MP3s for all the examples found in this book. Create playlists to study on the go or burn the sound files to a CD to listen at home. **The download link is found on the last page.**

We believe the best way to learn vocabulary—by far—is to study words within their proper context. Every idiom is followed by an example sentence and a paragraph or two explaining the context and usage.

Each idiom will have three sound files associated with it. The MP3s are all recorded by native voice actors and actresses.

The first sound file is the idiom itself. The second is the example sentence. The third sound file has the idiom, an English translation, the idiom repeated slowly, and the example sentence with translation. Try to mimic the Japanese speakers in sound and presentation.

We highly recommend knowing *hiragana* before tackling this book. Most words have *rōmaji*, but the example sentences do not. Every *kanji* here has *furigana* (small *hiragana*) over it to aid reading. If you do not yet know *hiragana*, please check out our *hiragana* book: "Hiragana, the Basics of Japanese."

Please download the sound files (link found on the last page). We hope this book by itself will be helpful, but the sound files give it an added value.

We have been involved with helping people learn (and teach) Japanese for over ten years now through our TheJapanesePage.com (free) website and TheJapanShop.com webstore. Please check those sites out!

Lastly, we would love to hear from you. If you have any suggestions to make this and other books better, please let us know.

Clay & Yumi Boutwell
help@thejapanshop.com
http://www.TheJapanShop.com
http://www.TheJapanesePage.com

あいづちを打つ

To throw in an appropriate word or sound of agreement (occasionally during a conversation)

- When talking with someone, to show you are engaged in the conversation, you may nod or say things like "That's right" or "You don't say!"
- Examples of あいづち *aizuchi* in Japanese are 「はい」 *hai,* 「うん」 *un,* 「へえ」 *hee,* and 「なるほど」 *naruhodo.*
- This idiom comes from the rhythm the blacksmith and his apprentice may have when trading blows hammering hot metal. The "*ai*" means "together" and "*tsuchi*" is a hammer. "*utsu*" means to hit. Two people hammering hot metal require careful coordination as do people in conversation.

EXAMPLE SENTENCE:

あの人の話は面白くなかったけれど、
一応あいづちを打ちながら聞
いていた。

That person's story was not interesting, but I listened while throwing in the occasional "uh huh" and "yes."

VOCABULARY:

あの人 *ano hito*—that person

話 *hanashi*—talk; story

面白くなかった *omoshiroku nakatta*—wasn't interesting

けれど *keredo*—but; however

一応 *ichiou*—for the time being; (sort of listened)

～ながら ~*nagara*—while (nodding)

聞いていた *kiiteita*—listened

Idiom 2

あけすけに言う

To say something frankly; openly; without reserve

- This idiom is used when someone says something in a blunt manner.
- "*ake*" means to begin or dawn; "*suke*" means to be transparent. Another, and probably the original, usage of "*akesuke*" is that a gap has opened up, and the other side is visible.

EXAMPLE SENTENCE:

あの人は、なんでもあけすけにいう。

That person always says things frankly.

VOCABULARY:

あの人 *ano hito*—that person
なんでも *nandemo*—anything; everything

Idiom 3

くち　おも
口が重い

To be slow to speak; tongue-tied

🛈 This is used when someone speaks only a little or is very quiet. The antonym of this expression is 口が軽い。 *kuchi ga karui.* One's mouth is light.

🛈 This idiom is literally, "mouth is heavy."

EXAMPLE SENTENCE:

さとう　　　　　　くち　おも
佐藤さんは、口が重いので、
ちゅう　　　　　　はな
デート中なにも話しませんでした。B

ecause Satou is naturally quiet, she didn't say anything during her date.

VOCABULARY:

佐藤 *satou*—Satou (a person's name)

ので *node*—therefore; because

デート中 *de-to chuu*—during a date

なにも *nanimo*—nothing; not at all

話しませんでした *hanashimasen deshita*—didn't speak

7

Idiom 4

くち　わ
口を割る

To confess; spill the beans; tell

- Very often this is used to get someone to confess a crime, but it can be used with any information, ideas, or secrets. A similar idiom (not in this collection) is 口が軽い *kuchi ga karui*. One's mouth is light (not heavy).
- Literally, "to divide the mouth in two." To make someone spill the beans, use 口を割らせる *kuchi wo waraseru* to draw out information; get someone to confess something.

EXAMPLE SENTENCE:

はんにん　　　　　　　　　　　くち　わ
犯人は、ようやく口を割った。

The criminal finally spilled the beans.

VOCABULARY:

犯人 *hannin*—the criminal; bad guy
ようやく *youyaku*—finally; at last; little by little

8

Idiom 5

くち　かた
口が堅い

To be tight-lipped; able to keep a secret; lips are sealed

- When someone never carelessly discloses information, they can be said to have a "hard" mouth. An antonym of this expression is 口が軽い。 *kuchi ga karui*. One's mouth is light (not heavy).
- Literally, "mouth is hard." Because a tight/hard mouth isn't likely to open, secrets are kept safe.

EXAMPLE SENTENCE:

かれ　　　くち　かた
彼は、口が堅いので、
ひみつ　　はな　　　　だいじょうぶ
秘密を話しても大丈夫だ。

He is pretty tight-lipped, so even telling him secrets is fine.

VOCABULARY:

彼 kare—he
ので node—therefore; because
秘密 himitsu—secret
話しても hanashitemo—even if (you) speak
大丈夫 daijoubu—OK; fine

Idiom 6

はら　わ
腹を割る

A heart-to-heart (talk); be frank

🛈 When you tell your innermost secrets without hiding anything, you are "splitting your belly." Compare this idiom with 口を割る。 *kuchi wo waru* - confess; spill the beans; tell (also in this collection)

🛈 Literally, "to split (one's) belly." Often in Japanese the belly (*hara*) is used idiomatically as the seat of thought or emotion when the English would be "heart." So to split one's belly is to have a "heart-to-heart" talk.

EXAMPLE SENTENCE:

きょう　　　　たが　　はら　わ　　　はな
今日は、お互いに腹を割って話そう。

Let's sit down for a heart-to-heart today.

VOCABULARY:

今日 *kyou*—today
お互いに *otagai ni*—together; each other
話そう *hanasou*—let's talk

Idiom 7

みみ いた
耳が痛い

To make one's ears burn; hit where it hurts

- When someone says something that hits on a touchy subject or reminds you of a weakness you have, then your "ears hurt."
- Literally, "ears hurt." The "hurt" in your ears comes from hearing something you don't want to hear.

EXAMPLE SENTENCE:

彼の忠告を聞くのは、耳が痛い。

Hearing his advice really hit a nerve.

VOCABULARY:

彼 *kare*—he
忠告 *chuukoku*—advice; counsel
聞く *kiku*—listen

Idiom 8

みみ
耳にたこができる

To be sick and tired of hearing something; to hear some-thing over and over again

- If someone "talks your ears off," instead of using this idiom, you can ignore them while claiming your "ears are far" (*mimi ga tooi*) which means you can't hear too well.
- Literally, "get calluses on one's ears." The "*tako*" here means "callus" such as what guitar players get on their fin-gers or the "corn" found on feet.
- Other common words with the same "tako" pronunciation are 1) 蛸 *tako* octopus and 2) 凧 *tako* kite (the toy you fly in the sky). The Mexican food, taco, is pronounced タコス *takosu*.

EXAMPLE SENTENCE:

しゅくだい
宿題をしなさいと、

みみ　　　　　　　　　　　　はは　い
耳にたこができるほど母に言われた。

My mother said, "Do your homework!" so many times my ears have developed calluses.

VOCABULARY:

宿題 *shukudai*—homework

しなさい *shinasai*—do (something)
[command]

と *to*—quotation marker

ほど *hodo*—to such an extent

母 *haha*—mother

言われた *iwareta*—said

Idiom 9

こみみ はさ
小耳に挟む

To happen to overhear something; little birdie told me...

- This is when you happen to overhear something and that information may or may not be accurate.
- Literally, "sandwich something between your small ears." The *komimi* (small ears) is probably only used with this idiom. Actually just saying *komimi* alone is used to mean "to overhear something."

EXAMPLE SENTENCE:

かのじょ ・ けっこん こみみ
彼女が結婚すると小耳にはさんだ。

A little birdie told me she is getting married.

VOCABULARY:

彼女 *kanojo*—she
結婚する *kekkon suru*—get married

Idiom 10

こころ
心 にかける

To keep close to one's heart; never forget; to take something to heart

- When someone is concerned with something or when there is something someone cannot forget, use this idiom.
- Literally, "hang in one's heart." Daijisen (a popular Japanese dictionary) lists "fall in love" and "do as one pleases" as alternate senses, but these may be archaic.

EXAMPLE SENTENCE:

ぼくし
あの牧師さんは、いつも

まず　　ひと　　　　こころ
貧しい人たちを 心 にかけている。

That pastor is always concerned with helping the poor.

VOCABULARY:

あの　*ano*—that
牧師　*bokushi*—pastor
いつも　*itsumo*—always
貧しい人たち *mazushii hito tachi*—poor people

Idiom 11

あげあしを取る

To find fault with someone

- This is used when someone makes fun of someone else's slip of the tongue or mistakes.
- "*Ageashi*" means "a raised leg" and refers to a sumo wrestler or martial artist executing a move by raising his leg. "*toru*" means "to take." So this phrase probably refers to grabbing the leg of your opponent as he exposes his weakness. When written in kanji, it is usually written as 揚げ足.

EXAMPLE SENTENCE:

原田さんは、人の揚げ足ばかり
取るので、楽しい会話ができない。

Since Harada is always making fun of the mistakes of others, it is hard to have a pleasant conversation.

VOCABULARY:

原田 *harada*—Harada (name)
人 *hito*—person
ばかり *bakari*—only; always (making fun)
ので *node*—therefore; because
楽しい *tanoshii*—fun
会話 *kaiwa*—conversation
できない *dekinai*—can't

Idiom 12

あご　ひと　つか
顎で人を使う

To push someone around

- This means to make someone do something in an arrogant manner.
- This idiom literally means "use people with your chin." Just using one's chin to direct someone to do something can be insulting.

EXAMPLE SENTENCE:

しゃちょう　　　　　ひと　つか
あの社長は、あごで人を使う。

That company president just pushes people around.

VOCABULARY:

あの *ano*—that
社長 *shachou*—(company) president

Idiom 13

<ruby>馬<rt>うま</rt></ruby>が<ruby>合<rt>あ</rt></ruby>う

To get along (with someone); hit it off

- Use this when you are on the same wavelength with someone else.
- Literally, "to suit a horse." This idiom comes from how a rider synchronizes his breathing to the horse's.

EXAMPLE SENTENCE:

<ruby>彼女<rt>かのじょ</rt></ruby>とは、<ruby>初<rt>はじ</rt></ruby>めて<ruby>会<rt>あ</rt></ruby>ったときから<ruby>馬<rt>うま</rt></ruby>があうと<ruby>感<rt>かん</rt></ruby>じた。

Upon meeting her for the first time, I just knew we'd hit it off.

VOCABULARY:

彼女 *kanojo*—she
初めて会ったとき *hajimete atta toki*—the first time (we) met
から *kara*—from (the first meeting)

と感じた *to kanjita*—had a feeling

Idiom 14

おお　　　かお
大きな顔をする

To look as if one is important; puffed up

- Said when someone is overly proud (and the speaker thinks that he should be more humble).
- Literally, "to make one's face large." Having a large face means people are more likely to take notice of you.

EXAMPLE SENTENCE:

かれ　　　　　　しんにゅうしゃいん
彼はまだ新入社員なのに
　　　　　おお　　　かお
もう大きな顔をしている。

He sure acts important for a new employee.

VOCABULARY:

彼　*kare*—he
まだ　*mada*—still (only a new employee)
新入社員　*shinnyuu shain*—new employee
なのに　*na noni*—although; in spite of...
もう　*mou*—already

Idiom 15

おんど と
音頭を取る

To lead a group of people; run the show

- This is literally to lead a group in singing, but can be for any purpose requiring a leader.
- "*Ondo*" are workmen's or marching songs.

EXAMPLE SENTENCE:

わたし　　　かんぱい　　　おんど
私が乾杯の音頭を
とらせていただきます。

Allow me to lead the toast.

VOCABULARY:

私 *watashi*—I

乾杯 *kanpai*—(drinking) toast

いただきます *itadakimasu*—literally "to receive" or "accept," this is used to show the leader's willingness to lead the toast.

Idiom 16

かお ひろ
顔が広い

To be well known; well connected

- Use this idiom to describe someone who has many acquaintances or connections.
- Literally, "face is wide." Having a large circle of friends and acquaintances means your face is "wide."

EXAMPLE SENTENCE:

ゆうめいじん
あんな有名人としりあいだなんて、

かお ひろ
顔が広いんですね。

For you to know such a famous person, you must have a
thick Rolodex.

VOCABULARY:

あんな *anna*—such (a famous person)
有名人 *yuumei jin*—a famous person
しりあい *shiriai*—an acquaintance
なんて *nante*—such as (knowing famous people)

21

Idiom 17

白羽の矢を立てる
しらは　や　た

To single someone out; mark someone out for (a position, mission)

- 🔘 This is said when someone is picked out of a large number (usually) of people for something special.
- 🔘 Literally, "establish a white-feathered arrow." Originally, this may have come from picking a victim (for a sacrifice). A white feathered arrow would mysteriously stick up from a roof to show which young girl should be the victim.

EXAMPLE SENTENCE:

次期社長候補として、
じ　き　しゃちょうこうほ

吉田さんに白羽の矢をたてた。
よしだ　　　　しらは　や

Yoshida was the candidate chosen for the next company president.

VOCABULARY:

次期 *jiki*—next term; the following...
社長 *shachou*—(company) president
候補 *kouho*—candidacy
として *toshite*—as; in the capacity of...

吉田 *yoshida*—Yoshida (name)

Idiom 18

あ
そりが合わない

Unable to hit it off; not get along; unable to cooperate

- When people's personality or ways of thinking are not compatible. The opposite of this would be 馬が合う *uma ga au* - "to get along (with someone)." (This is also found in this collection)
- This comes from the *sori* (curve) of a katana (Japanese sword) not fitting (*awanai*) its scabbard.

EXAMPLE SENTENCE:

た な か
田中さんは、上司とそりがあわない
じょうし
かいしゃ
といって会社をやめた。

Tanaka quit, saying he couldn't get along with his superiors.

VOCABULARY:

田中 *tanaka*—Tanaka (name)
上司 *joushi*—one's superiors; higher-ups
会社 *kaishi*—company
やめた *yameta*—quit

Idiom 19

み かた
身を固める

To settle down; get married and raise a family

- ● This can be a synonym for marriage. Use only with men.
- ● The original meaning may have been to armor oneself, which evolved into putting ones attire in order.

EXAMPLE SENTENCE:

おい、君、そろそろ身をかためたらどうか？
Hey, shouldn't you start thinking about settling down?

VOCABULARY:

おい *oi*—Hey! (can be a little rude)
君 *kimi*—you
そろそろ *sorosoro*—soon; to be about time for...
どうか *dou ka*—how about...?

Idiom 20

目をかける
め

To look after; take care of...; be kind to...; to favor

- The object of one's attention is marked by に.
- Literally, "hang one's eyes (on something)." Because one's eyes are connected to that someone or something, it means "take care of."

EXAMPLE SENTENCE:

しんらい
信頼できるので、

しゃちょう　かれ　め
社長は彼に目をかけています。

Because he is trustworthy, the company president favors him.

VOCABULARY:

信頼 *shinrai*—trust; confidence
できる *dekiru*—can; able to
ので *node*—therefore; because
社長 *shachou*—(company) president
彼 *kare*—he

Idiom 21

けんえん　なか
犬猿の仲

To be on bad terms; hate each other's guts; fight like cats and dogs

- When you just can't get along with someone, your relationship is like that of a dog (*ken*) and monkey (*en*).
- "The relationship between dogs and monkeys." This saying came about because dogs and monkeys do not naturally get along.

EXAMPLE SENTENCE:

ふたり　あ
あの二人は会ったらすぐにけんかを
けんえん　なか
はじめてしまう。犬猿の仲だ。T

hose two start bickering as soon as they meet. Just like cats and dogs.

VOCABULARY:

あの二人 *ano futari*—those two (people)
会ったら *attara*—if (they) meet; upon meeting
すぐに *sugu ni*—soon
けんか *kenka*—fight; bickering

はじめてしまう *hajimete shimau*—(unfortunately) start (fighting)

27

Idiom 22

ちから　か
力を貸す

To lend someone a hand; help out

- Use the particle の *no* to show whose "power" will be lent. Ex. *anata no~* (your help); *watashi no~* (my help); *tanaka no~* (Tanaka's help)
- Literally, "lend power." Just as we say "to lend a hand," in Japanese it is "to lend power or strength."

EXAMPLE SENTENCE:

しごと　せいこう
この仕事を成功させるために、
ちから　か
ぜひあなたの力を貸してほしい。

In order to make this project a success, I really want your help.

VOCABULARY:

この仕事 *kono shigoto*—this case; this matter
成功させる *seikou saseru*—to make (it) a success
ために *tame ni*—for that reason
ぜひ *zehi*—by all means
あなたの *anata no*—your
ほしい *hoshii*—want

Idiom 23

ち　　なみだ
血も 涙もない

Cold-blooded; hardhearted; unfeeling; inhuman

- Use when someone is cold, unfeeling, or insusceptible to pity.
- Literally, "without blood or tears." A similar expression is 人 でなし *hitode nashi* - inhuman; a brute; a monster.

EXAMPLE SENTENCE:

ひと　　ころ
こんなやさしい人を殺すなんて、

はんにん　ち　なみだ
犯人は血も 涙もないやつだ。

To have killed such a nice person, the murderer must be inhuman.

VOCABULARY:

こんな *konna*—such as this...
やさしい *yasashii*—kind
人 *hito*—person
殺す *korosu*—kill
なんて *nante*—such as (killing people)
犯人 *hannin*—bad guy; the offender
やつ *yatsu*—guy; fellow (usually with a negative feel)

Idiom 24

後ろ指を指される

うし　ゆび　さ

To be talked about behind one's back; insult someone behind his back

- Use this when someone is the object of finger pointing.
- Someone behind you is pointing at you.

EXAMPLE SENTENCE:

嘘ばかりついていると、人から
後ろ指を指されるようになるぞ。

Keep lying like that and pretty soon people will be talking about you behind your back.

VOCABULARY:

嘘 *uso*—a lie; a fib
〜ばかり *~bakari*—only; always (lying)
ついている *tsuiteiru*—to tell (a lie)
人から *hito kara*—from people
ようになる *you ni naru*—will become like...

Idiom 25

うら か
恨みを買う

To incur someone's ill will; to make an enemy

- This is used when someone does something (even unintentional) that causes someone to be envious or spiteful.
- Literally, "to buy hard feelings." But the "*kau*" (to buy) means "to solicit" the hard feelings instead of anything to do with money.

EXAMPLE SENTENCE:

わたし   うら
私には、あなたから恨み

か   おぼ
を買った覚えはない。

I don't remember doing anything to make you mad at me.

VOCABULARY:

私 *watashi*—I
あなたから *anata kara*—from you
覚えはない *oboe wa nai*—(I) don't recall; have
no recollection

Idiom 26

えんぎ　わる
縁起が悪い

Bad luck; bad omen; unlucky

ⓘ **縁起** *engi* is used like the English "luck"; it can be "good" or "bad." Literally, "an omen is bad."

EXAMPLE SENTENCE:

あさ　で　　　　　　　　くつひも
朝、出かけるときに靴紐が

き　　　　　　　　　　えんぎ　わる
切れてしまうなんて、縁起が悪い。

This morning, my shoelace broke when I left home. I must have bad luck.

VOCABULARY:

朝 *asa*—morning
出かけるとき *dekakeru toki*—when leaving
靴紐 *kutsu himo*—shoelace
切れてしまう *kirete shimau*—(unfortunately) broke (shoelace)
なんて *nante*—such as (things such as breaking shoelaces)

Idiom 27

かお　　　　　ひ　　　　で
顔から火が出る

To burn with shame; be embarrassed

- Use this idiom when your face turns bright red from extreme embarrassment.
- Literally, "fire comes out of the face." This idiom comes from describing a very red—and embarrassed—face. We might associate flames with anger, but this idiom means to be "embarrassed."
- Also see 穴があったら入りたい *ana ga attara hairitai*. If there was a hole, I'd like to crawl in it (in embarrassment).

EXAMPLE SENTENCE:

ひとまえ　　　ころ
たくさんの人前で転んでしまい、
かお　　　　ひ
顔から火がでた。

I tripped and fell in front of a lot of people and my face turned bright red (in embarrassment).

VOCABULARY:

たくさん　*takusan*—many
人前　*hito mae*—in front of people
転んでしまい　*koronde shimai*—(unfortunately) fall

Idiom 28

くちぐるま　　　の
口車に乗る

To fall for someone's line; be cajoled; be taken in by someone's sweet talk

- Use this with people who are easily flattered or easily led to believe the unbelievable.
- The use of "*noru*" for "to be carried away" or "get fooled into joining..." is common in Japanese.

EXAMPLE SENTENCE:

あのおばあさんは、詐欺師の口車に乗って大金を騙し取られてしまった。

That old woman was taken in by a swindler who cajoled her into giving him a lot of money.

VOCABULARY:

あの *ano*—that
おばあさん *obaasan*—old lady
詐欺師 *sagishi*—a swindler; a crook
大金 *tai kin*—a large amount of money
騙し取られて *damashi torarete*—to have taken away by trickery

34

Idiom 29

ゴマすり

Kissing up; overly flattering; sucking up

- In the US, people may make smooching sounds to mean "kiss up." But in Japan, people rub their fist over the palm of their other hand in a grinding motion. This is to imitate the action of "grinding sesame."
- When boiled sesame (*goma*) is ground in a grinding bowl, bits of sesame stick here and there. This may resemble how flattery can "stick" to some people.

EXAMPLE SENTENCE:

彼は、ゴマすりがうまいので、会社で出世した。

He got promoted for being really talented at kissing up.

VOCABULARY:

彼 *kare*—he
うまい *umai*—good at
ので *node*—therefore; because
会社 *kaisha*—company

出世 *shusse*—promotion

Idiom 30

白い目で見る
しろ　　め　　み

To give the cold shoulder; look coldly at...

- When looking down on people coldly and with evil intent.
- Literally, "to look with the white of one's eyes." This is a variation of 白眼視 *hakuganshi* which means "to frown upon someone; look coldly upon someone; etc."

EXAMPLE SENTENCE:

刑務所から出てきたばかりの人は、
世間から白い目で見られる。

A person recently released from jail is looked down upon by society.

VOCABULARY:

刑務所 *keimusho*—prison
から *kara*—from
出てきたばかり *dete kita bakari*—just left (prison)
人 *hito*—person
世間 *seken*—the world; society
から *kara*—from

Idiom 31

ねこ　　かぶ
猫を被る

To feign friendliness; hide one's true feelings; play the innocent

- When you pretend to be one thing when you really are something else, you "wear a cat."
- Literally, "to wear a cat." This may have come about because a cat on the outside seems to be gentle, but inside the cat is wily and devious.

EXAMPLE SENTENCE:

かのじょ
いつもはおてんばな彼女だが、
す　　　ひと　　まえ　　　ねこ
好きな人の前では猫をかぶっておとな
しくしていた。

She's such a tomboy, but she sure acted like a lady around that guy she likes.

VOCABULARY:

いつも *itsumo*—always
おてんば *otenba*—tomboyishness
彼女 *kanojo*—she
が *ga*—but; however
好きな人 *suki na hito*—the person (she) likes
の前で *no mae de*—in front of...
おとなしくしていた *otonashiku shiteita*—became
very gentle

Idiom 32

は　　く
歯を食いしばる

Grin and bear; clench one's jaw

- A common word in Japanese (culture as well as language) is 我慢 *gaman* which means "self-control; bear; patience." This phrase is to "*gaman*" extreme pain or anger.
- Literally, "to grit one's teeth."

EXAMPLE SENTENCE:

ぐんたい　　とっくん　　は　　く　　　　　た
軍隊の特訓に歯を食いしばって耐えた。

The soldiers clenched their teeth and endured the special exercises.

VOCABULARY:

軍隊 *guntai*—armed forces
特訓 *tokkun*—special training; exercises
耐えた *taeta*—endured

Idiom 33

はな
鼻につく

To be disgusted with; sick and tired of...; fed up with...

- No matter how much you like something, too much of it will make it less desirable.
- Literally, "stick to one's nose" (like an unpleasant odor.)

EXAMPLE SENTENCE:

あの人の話し方は、きどっていて鼻につく。

I can't stand the way that person talks with such conceit.

VOCABULARY:

あの人 *ano hito*—that person
話し方 *hanashi kata*—the way (he) talks
きどっていて *kidotteite*—putting on airs; be snobbish

Idiom 34

はら　くろ
腹が黒い

Black hearted; mean-spirited

- When someone by all appearances seems to be nice, but deep inside is really a mean-spirited grump, he can be said to have a "black stomach."
- The phrase apparently was inspired by a fish called サヨリ (Japanese halfbeak, Sayori). This fish is known for its slim and beautiful shape. But if you look at the fish closely, it has a black streak running down its stomach. Therefore, a "black stomach" reveals the beast within the beauty.

EXAMPLE SENTENCE:

せいじか　　はら　くろ
あの政治家は腹が黒い。

That politician is black-hearted.

VOCABULARY:

あの *ano*—that
政治家 *seijika*—politician

Idiom 35

ふくろ
袋のネズミ

A mouse in a trap; to be cornered; in a tight situation

- When you are trapped, cornered, and have no way out.
- Literally, "a bagged mouse." When a mouse is tricked into running into a bag, there is no escape.

EXAMPLE SENTENCE:

ふくろ
お前はもう袋のネズミだ。

You are trapped now.

VOCABULARY:

お前 *omae*—you
もう *mou*—now; as of now

Idiom 36

あし　ぼう
足が棒になる

To walk one's legs off; have very sore legs; my dogs are barking

- Have you ever walked so much your legs feel like boards? Next time that happens, say, "*ashi ga bou ni natta.*"
- Literally, "legs became staffs." This comes from tired legs getting as stiff as a board.

EXAMPLE SENTENCE:

いちにちじゅうある　　　　　あし　ぼう
一日中歩いたので、足が棒になった。

I walked all day, and now my legs are as stiff as a board.

VOCABULARY:

一日中 *ichinichi juu*—all day long
歩いた *aruita*—walked
ので *node*—therefore; because

Idiom 37

ねこ
猫ババ

To pocket something (that one finds); embezzle; take illegal possession of...

- Use this expression when someone finds something such as a lost wallet and picks it up without trying to find its owner.
- Literally, "cat poop." This probably comes from a cat kicking sand over its droppings to hide them. Similarly, an embezzler covers up his crime and pretends he has done nothing wrong.

EXAMPLE SENTENCE:

そんなにたくさんのお金をどうして
もっているんだ？まさか猫ばばし
たのか？

Why are you carrying all that cash? You didn't pick it up some-where, did you?

VOCABULARY:

そんなに *sonnani*—so much (cash)
たくさん *takusan*—much; a lot
お金 *okane*—money
どうして *doushite*—why

もっている *motteiru*—carrying
まさか *masaka*—surely!; impossible!

Idiom 38

たぬき寝入り

Pretending to be asleep; play possum

- Next time you pretend to sleep during class or act like you can't hear when someone is scolding you, think of this phrase.
- Literally, "a sleeping raccoon-dog." A *tanuki* sometimes faints or plays dead when it hears a gunshot even if it wasn't close to being shot. So when someone should be paying attention, that someone pretends to ignore it.

EXAMPLE SENTENCE:

私の夫は、たぬき寝入りがうまい。

My husband is great at pretending to be asleep.

VOCABULARY:

私の *watashi no*—my
夫 *otto*—husband
うまい *umai*—good at...

Idiom 39

あかご て
赤子の手をひねるよう

Something very easy; taking candy from a baby

- This is used when someone from a position of strength does as he pleases with someone weaker. This is probably most often used with bad guys doing something bad to the weak and defenseless.
- Literally, "like twisting a child's arm." This idiom seems to have an obvious origin: twisting a small child's arm is not difficult.

EXAMPLE SENTENCE:

けいさんもんだい　と
こんな計算問題を解くのは、

あかご　て
赤子の手をひねるようだ。

Solving a math problem like this is child's play.

VOCABULARY:

こんな *konna*—such as this
計算問題 *keisan mondai*—math problem
解く *toku*—solve (math problem)

Idiom 40

あと　まつ
後の祭り

Too late; can't do anything after the fact

- This idiom is used when one regrets losing a chance to do something.
- One possible origin of this phrase is from a float in a Kyoto festival. When it arrives with great fanfare, this is called "*mae no matsuri*" (before the festival), but when it leaves (*ato no matsuri*), not many people are there. With the festival being less festive, they missed the boat.

EXAMPLE SENTENCE:

しけん　　　　　　　お
試験はもう終わってしまった。
いまごろべんきょう　　　　　　あと
今頃勉強しても後のまつりだ。

The test is over. Studying now will do no good.

VOCABULARY:

試験 *shiken*—test
もう *mou*—now; as of now
終わってしまった *owatte shimatta*—all over; finished
今頃 *ima goro*—about this time; now
勉強しても *benkyou shitemo*—even if (you) study

Idiom 41

鵜の目・鷹の目
う　　め　　たか　　め

Keen eyes; vigilant; attentive

- Eyes sharp as a bird.
- "*u*" is a type of bird with a long neck (cormorant) and "*taka*" is a falcon. Both are excellent at hunting prey thus inspiring the "vigilant" meaning.

EXAMPLE SENTENCE:

あの刑事は、犯人の手がかりがないか
と鵜の目、鷹の目で探し回って
いる。

That detective is combing the scene with a fine tooth brush to see if any clues were left by the criminal.

VOCABULARY:

あの刑事 *ano keiji*—that detective
犯人 *hannin*—bad guy; criminal
手がかり *tegakari*—clue
ないかと *nai ka to*—(to see) if there are any (clues) or not
探し回っている *sagashi mawatte iru*—looking around

Idiom 42

うんでい　さ
雲泥の差

A world of difference; all the difference in the world

- This may be used to describe two things that truly are worlds apart but some people may superficially think of them as being similar.
- Literally, "the difference between clouds and dirt." Because the phrase compares "sky" with "dirt," there may be an implication of one being good and the other bad (dirt).

EXAMPLE SENTENCE:

ほんもの
本物のダイヤモンドと、

にせもの　　　かがや　　うんでい　さ
ガラスの偽物とでは輝きに雲泥の差がある。

The glitter of a real diamond is worlds apart from that of a glass fake.

VOCABULARY:

本物 *honmono*—the real thing; genuine
ダイヤモンド *daiyamondo*—diamond
ガラス *garasu*—glass
偽物 *nisemono*—a fake
輝き *kagayaki*—shine; glitter

Idiom 43

かげ　うす
影が薄い

In the background; not standing out

- To say someone (or something) has lost some influence, add "*naru*" as in: *kage ga usukunatta.* (His) influence has waned.
- Literally, "shadow is pale/weak." Someone doesn't cast as long of a shadow.

EXAMPLE SENTENCE:

すずき　　　　　きょうしつ　　　かげ　うす　そんざい
鈴木さんは、教室では影が薄い存在だが、
　　　　やきゅうぶ　　　かつやく
野球部では活躍している。

Suzuki is almost invisible in the classroom, but very active in the baseball club.

VOCABULARY:

鈴木 *suzuki*—Suzuki (a name)
教室 *kyou shitsu*—a classroom
存在 *sonzai*—existence; being
が *ga*—but; however

野球部 *yakyuubu*—baseball club
活躍 *katsuyaku*—active

Idiom 44

くび
首をひねる

To tilt one's head in puzzlement; think hard; rack one's brains; be baffled about...

- ❶ Use this when baffled by a puzzle or problem or with something that requires hard thought.
- ❶ Literally, "to twist one's neck." When puzzled people tend to tilt their necks.

EXAMPLE SENTENCE:

てんさい　　　　　　　　がくせい
天才といわれた学生も、

もんだい　　　くび
この問題には首をひねった。

Even the "genius" student scratched his head about this problem.

VOCABULARY:

天才 *tensai*—genius
といわれた *to iwareta*—it is said...
学生 *gakusei*—student
も *mo*—even; also
この問題 *kono mondai*—this problem

Idiom 45

ず   の
図に乗る

To get carried away (with success); overplay one's hand; push a good thing too far; press one's luck

- To say "Don't push your luck!" or "Don't get carried away!" use 図に乗るな。 *zu ni noru na.*
- Also written as 頭に乗る *atama ni noru* to go to one's head.

EXAMPLE SENTENCE:

せんせい   こ   ず   の
先生、あの子がすぐに図に乗らない

ときどききび
ように、時々厳しくしかってくだ

さい。

Teacher, please be stern at times, so my child won't get carried away by a little bit of success.

VOCABULARY:

先生 *sensei*—teacher
あの子 *ano ko*—my child (lit. that child)
すぐに *sugu ni*—soon; immediately; in no time
ないように *nai you ni*—so it won't happen
時々 *tokidoki*—sometimes
厳しく *kibishiku*—sternly
しかってください *shikatte kudasai*—please scold;
please chide

Idiom 46

地におちる

To fall into decline; be brought low

- When someone's reputation, strength, etc is brought really low.
- Literally, "falls to the ground."

EXAMPLE SENTENCE:

こんな不祥事が起こっては、

わが社の名声は地に落ちたも同然だ。

Having this scandal happen is as good as ruining our company's reputation.

VOCABULARY:

こんな *konna*—such as this
不祥事 *fushouji*—scandal
起こって *okotte*—happened; occurred
わが社 *wagasha*—our company
名声 *meisei*—good name; fame
同然 *douzen*—the same as; as good as...

Idiom 47

根も葉もない
ね　は

Unfounded rumor; groundless

- This is usually used with rumors or gossip.
- Literally, "has neither root nor leaf." Without the root, the plant can't live or stand. As a result there can't be any leaves either.

EXAMPLE SENTENCE:

そんなことを信じるな。
しん

根も葉もないうわさだ。
ね　は

Don't believe that. It's nothing but an unfounded rumor.

VOCABULARY:

そんなこと *sonna koto*—something such as that
信じるな *shinjiru na*—don't believe
うわさ *uwasa*—rumor

Idiom 48

ひとすじなわ
一筋縄ではいかない

Very hard to manage; difficult to handle

- Use this when you are faced with a problem and the only possible solution is very difficult.
- Literally, "won't work with one piece of rope." The "*hitosuji*" literally means a piece of rope, but another meaning is "ordinary means/method." To get out of a tight situation, two or three pieces of ropes would be better, but there is only one piece of rope.

EXAMPLE SENTENCE:

せいじ　せかい　　　ひとすじなわ　　　　　　もんだい　おお
政治の世界は、一筋縄ではいかない問題が多い。

In the world of politics, there are many hard-to-handle
problems.

VOCABULARY:

政治の世界 *seiji no sekai*—the world of politics
問題 *mondai*—problem
多い *ooi*—many

Idiom 49

まと　い
的を射る

To be to the point; relevant (remark)

- When someone says something that hits the nail on the head, use this. Used with speech or written word. An antonym is 的を外れる *mato o hazureru* to miss the mark.
- Literally, "shoot the target." This came from hitting the bull's eye (*mato*) with an arrow (射る *iru* is the verb used for shooting an arrow).

EXAMPLE SENTENCE:

かれ　こた　まと　い
彼の答えは的を射ていたので、

はんろん
だれも反論しなかった。

His answer was right on mark, so no one gave a counter argument.

VOCABULARY:

彼 *kare*—he
答え *kotae*—an answer
ので *node*—therefore; because
だれも *dare mo*—no one
反論 *hanron*—a counterargument; a refutation
しなかった *shinakatta*—there wasn't (a counter argument)

Idiom 50

あさめしまえ
朝飯前

Child's play; cinch; no sweat; piece of cake

- This is a fancy way to say, 簡単 *kantan*—easy.
- Literally, "before breakfast." Because breakfast is usually one of the first activities of the day, the time before breakfast is short. Only easy things can be accomplished during that time.

EXAMPLE SENTENCE:

しょうがくせい　　しゅくだい　　てつだ
小学生の宿題を手伝うなんて、

こうこうせい　　ぼく　　あさめしまえ
高校生の僕には朝飯前だ。

Helping an elementary school kid with his homework is no sweat for a high schooler like me.

VOCABULARY:

小学生 *shougakusei*—elementary school child
宿題 *shukudai*—homework
手伝う *tetsudau*—help
なんて *nante*—such as this
高校生 *koukousei*—high school student
ぼく *boku*—I
高校生の僕には *koukousei no boku ni wa*—for a highschooler like me

Idiom 51

ねこ　ひたい
猫の 額 ほど

Tiny; size of a cat's forehead

- This is often used for the size of land, a room, or any other space.
- Literally, "no more than the size of a cat's forehead."

EXAMPLE SENTENCE:

ねこ　　ひたい　　　　　　　　　はたけ
猫の 額 ほどしかない 畑 でも、

やさい　　と
おいしい野菜が取れる。 Even a tiny parcel of land can produce delicious vegetables.

VOCABULARY:

しかない *shikanai*—only (a small piece of land)

畑 *hatake*—garden; plot for vegetables

でも *demo*—even

おいしい *oishii*—delicious

野菜 *yasai*—vegetables

取れる *toreru*—can bring forth (vegetables)

Idiom 52

まく　と
幕を閉じる

Ending; to put an end to

- An opposite is 幕を開く *maku wo aku* to open the curtain; begin.
- Literally, "to close the curtain." This originated from the closing of the curtain at the end of a play.

EXAMPLE SENTENCE:

えいが　　　　　　　　　　　　　　まく　と
その映画は、ハッピーエンドで幕を閉じた。

That movie finished with a happy ending.

VOCABULARY:

その映画 *sono eiga*—that movie
ハッピーエンド *happi-endo*—a happy ending

Idiom 53

あたま　あ
頭が上がらない

To be no match for...; be overwhelmed by someone; be indebted

- When someone feels inferior (whether from shame or awe) or when someone is indebted somehow to someone else.
- Literally, "can't lift one's head." This idiom probably comes from hanging one's head down in shame or unworthiness.

EXAMPLE SENTENCE:

かいしゃ　いちばん　い　ば　　　　　　しゃちょう
会社で一番威張っている社長だが、

いえ　　　おく　　　　あたま
家では奥さんに頭が上がらない。

At the company, the president throws his weight around,
but at home his wife is the boss.

VOCABULARY:

会社で *kaisha de*—at the company; around the office
一番 *ichiban*—#1; the most...; ~est
威張っている *ibatteiru*—throw one's weight around; high-handedly
社長 *shachou*—(company) president
家で *ie de*—at home
奥さん *okusan*—wife

Idiom 54

裏をかく
うら

To outsmart; counterplot; outmaneuver

- When someone expects one thing, but receives the opposite; to outwit or fool one's opponent into not expecting something.
- This idiom came from piercing the inside (*ura*) of some-one's armor through an opening or weak-spot. "*Ura*" is often used idiomatically as "hidden" such as with 裏技 *urawaza*—a hidden trick or tip; 裏を読む *ura wo yomu*—to *read* between the lines.

EXAMPLE SENTENCE:

私は、相手の作戦の裏をかいて勝った。

I outmaneuvered my opponent and won.

VOCABULARY:

私 *watashi*—I
相手 *aite*—opponent; the other side
作戦 *sakusen*—strategy
勝った *katta*—won

Idiom 55

かお
顔をたてる

To save face

- When you want to protect someone from embarrassment, you are "holding up their face."
- Literally, "to stand up (someone's) face." This is similar to the English idiom "to save face."

EXAMPLE SENTENCE:

あいて　　かお
相手の顔をたててあなたが

あやま
謝ってください。

Apologize and let him save face.

VOCABULARY:

相手 *aite*—1) partner; companion 2) opponent; the other side
あなた *anata*—you
謝ってください *ayamattekudasai*—please apologize

Idiom 56

かた　　　も
肩を持つ

To side with; take sides; support (something)

- When you want to support someone, you can say you are "holding (up) their shoulders"
- Literally, "hold shoulders." When you hold someone's shoulders, you support them so they can stand erect.

EXAMPLE SENTENCE:

てき　　かた　　も
あなたは敵の肩を持つのか？

Are you thinking of taking the enemy's side?

VOCABULARY:

あなた *anata*—you
敵 *teki*—enemy
か *ka*—question marker

Idiom 57

かぶと^ぬを脱ぐ

To admit defeat; give up

- To recognize someone's superiority in something.
- Literally, "remove helmet." Removing one's helmet was a way for a warrior to admit defeat. A similar phrase is シャッポを脱ぐ *shappo o nuku* - to take one's hat off. (to admit one's inferiority) This is not used as often today as *kabuto o nugu*, though.

EXAMPLE SENTENCE:

彼の猛勉強振りには、

かぶとを脱ぐよ。

I take my hat off (admit defeat) to his diligent studying.

VOCABULARY:

彼 *kare*—he
猛勉強 *mou benkyou*—studying hard
～振り ˜*buri*—the appearance of (studying hard)

65

Idiom 58

きゃっこう　　　あ
脚光を浴びる

To take center stage

- When someone or something is brought out into everyone's attention.
- Literally, "to bathe in the limelight (footlights)."

EXAMPLE SENTENCE:

じょゆう　　　　めいえんぎ　　きゃっこう　　　あ
あの女優は、名演技で脚光を浴びた。
That actress bathed in the limelight of her fine performance.

VOCABULARY:

あの女優 *ano joyuu*—that actress
名演技 *meiengi*—good acting; excellent performance
脚光 *kyakkou*—footlights
浴びた *abita*—bathed

Idiom 59

くちび き
口火を切る

To start; begin; trigger; light the spark that...

- ❶ This phrase tends to be used with war-like imagery: actual battles, arguments, or big incidents.
- ❶ Literally, "to cut a fuse." This probably came about from the lighting of the fuse connected to an old-fashioned gun. The spark that caused the gun to fire "started the battle."

EXAMPLE SENTENCE:

あのときのあのうそが大事件の口火を切った。

That lie back then was what triggered the serious incident.

VOCABULARY:

あのとき　*ano toki*—that time (back then)
あのうそ　*ano uso*—that lie (back then)
大事件　*daijiken*—a big event; serious matter

Idiom 60

たかをくくる

To make light of...; think little of...; to not take something seriously

- This is often used when something that should be given more importance is taken lightly.
- The "*taka*" (高) means "an amount or quantity of something" and the "*kukuru*" (括) means "to put it all together" as a kind of loose estimate. Because great care wasn't taken to count precisely, it came to mean "to make light of."

EXAMPLE SENTENCE:

敵はもう攻めてこないとたかを
くくっている。今がチャンスだ。

The enemy isn't taking the possibility of an attack seriously.
Now is our chance.

VOCABULARY:

敵 *teki*—enemy
もう *mou*—no longer; not any more
攻めてこない *semete konai*—won't come and
attack
今 *ima*—now
チャンス *chansu*—chance

Idiom 61

とうかく　あらわ
頭角を現す

To distinguish oneself; stand out; be in the forefront

🛈 This is usually used to refer to someone else's (not oneself) talent or ability.

🛈 Literally, "shows the top of his head." The top of the class (what sticks up at the top) of the arts, science, and other talents.

EXAMPLE SENTENCE:

かれ　　　　すうがく　　とうかく　　あらわ
彼は、数学で頭角を現した。

He distinguished himself in mathematics.

VOCABULARY:

彼 *kare*—he
数学 *suugaku*—mathematics

Idiom 62

は　　　　た
歯が立たない

Unable to compete; bite off more than one can chew; be too much for one; difficult

- In addition to this idiomatic usage, "*ha ga tatanai*" is also used to mean "can't bite" (because something is too hard)—この せんべいは硬くて歯が立たない。*kono senbei wa katakute ha ga tatanai.* This *senbei* (Japanese rice cracker) is so hard, I can't bite it.
- Literally, "teeth won't stand."

EXAMPLE SENTENCE:

ボクシングのチャンピオンにけんか

か　　　　　　　　　　むり
で勝とうとしても無理だ。とても

は　た
歯が立たない。

It is impossible (even if you try) to beat a boxing champion in a fight. That's just biting off more than you can chew.

VOCABULARY:

ボクシング *bokushingu*—boxing
チャンピオン *chanpion*—champion
けんか *kenka*—fight
勝とう *katou*—to fight
としても *toshitemo*—even if, even though...
無理 *muri*—impossible
とても *totemo*—very

Idiom 63

ばんじきゅう
万事休す

Nothing more can be done; the jig is up; game over

- This can be used when just about anything is ending (sports, work, school, relationships, etc)
- Literally, "all things stop." This is from a Chinese saying. The "*banji*" means "everything" and "*kyuusu*" here means "to end" (with the kanji 休 for "rest").

EXAMPLE SENTENCE:

ぜんぜん　　かね　　　　　　ばんじきゅう
もう全然お金がない。万事休すだ。

There is no more money. We are done for.

VOCABULARY:

もう *mou*—not any longer; no longer
全然 *zenzen*—(none) at all [used with a negative verb]
お金 *okane*—money

Idiom 64

あぶら　　の
脂 が乗る

Warm up to one's work; get into the swing of things

- Another meaning for this phrase is "delicious" and usually refers to eating fish.
- Literally, "fat rides." An idiom dictionary lists two other senses for this phrase: fish being rich in fat, and a woman's skin being flexible and moist at the prime of her life.

EXAMPLE SENTENCE:

しけんべんきょう　　あぶら　　の
試験勉強に脂が乗ってきた。

I finally got into the studying groove.

VOCABULARY:

試験勉強 *shiken benkyou*—studying for a test

Idiom 65

痛くも痒くもない
（いた）（かゆ）

No skin off my back; not my concern; I couldn't care less

- Used when showing unconcern about anything.
- Literally, "No pain or itchiness"

EXAMPLE SENTENCE:

あなたに何を言われても、
（なに）（い）

痛くも痒くもない。
（いた）（かゆ）

Whatever you have to say, it makes no difference to me.

VOCABULARY:

あなた *anata*—you
何を言われても *nani o iwaretemo*—no matter whatever you say

Idiom 66

いた　　　つ
板に付く

To become second nature; become comfortable; be at home with; in one's element

- This refers to someone's attitude, manner, clothing, work, etc.
- The board here "*ita*" refers to the floor of a stage. And the "*tsuku*" probably means "to fit well" (with the stage). It probably originated from an actor or actress who is at home on the stage.

EXAMPLE SENTENCE:

かのじょ　　　　こうこう　　にゅうがく　　　　はんとし
彼女は、高校に入学して半年たったので、

せいふくすがた　　いた
制服姿が板についてきた。

Since she's been in high school now for half a year, she has gotten used to her uniform.

VOCABULARY:

彼女 *kanojo*—she
高校 *koukou*—high school
入学 *nyuugaku*—entering school
半年 *hantoshi*—half a year
ので *node*—therefore; because
制服姿 *seifuku sugata*—(her) appearance in a uniform

Idiom 67

味をしめる
あじ

To develop a taste for...; to be encouraged by initial success

- A useful example one might hear in a potato chip ad is 「一度味をしめたらやめられない。」 *ichido aji o shimetara yamerarenai.* If you try it once, you won't be able to stop.
- The *"aji"* means "taste" and *"shimeru"* probably means, "experience" here. Having tasted something really good, a person comes back to it expecting the same tastiness.

EXAMPLE SENTENCE:

一度ついたうそがばれなかったので、

味をしめた彼はうそばかりついている。

He told one lie and got away with it. Having developed a taste for it, he lies all the time now.

VOCABULARY:

一度 *ichido*—once
ついたうそ *tsuita uso*—a lie told
ばれなかった *barenakatta*—didn't get caught
ので *node*—therefore; because

彼 *kare*—he
うそ *uso*—lie
〜ばかり ˜*bakari*—only; always (lying)
ついている *tsuite iru*—telling (lies)

Idiom 68

ふた
うり二つ

Two peas in a pod; spitting image

- Used to refer to the resemblance between parent and child or between siblings.
- Literally, "two (alike) melons." This idiom is said to be an abbreviation of a longer one meaning "like splitting a melon in half."

EXAMPLE SENTENCE:

わたし　　おとうと　　ふた
私は、弟とうり二つ

い
だとよく言われる。

People often say my brother and I are like two peas in a pod.

VOCABULARY:

私 watashi—I
弟 otouto—younger brother
よく yoku—often
言われる iwareru—they say...

Idiom 69

くび
首をつっこむ

To take part in; be interested in; be engrossed in

- ❶ This is usually used with an engrossing conversation (gossip, problem, something of interest).
- ❶ Literally, "thrust one's head into something." (首 can refer to "head" as well as "neck.")

EXAMPLE SENTENCE:

もんだい　　くび
そんなばかばかしい問題に首を
つっこまないほうがいい。

You shouldn't get involved with such a stupid problem.

VOCABULARY:

そんな *sonna*—such; like that
ばかばかしい *bakabakashii*—absurd; ridiculous; silly
問題 *mondai*—problem
ほうがいい *hou ga ii*—better (not to get involved)

Idiom 70

くび　　なが
首を長くする

Eagerly look forward to something

- Imagine stretching your neck out to look closely for something you are expecting to come.
- Literally, "make one's neck longer." It is similar to the English idiom, "to crane one's neck."

EXAMPLE SENTENCE:

かのじょ　　　　　かれ　　く
彼女は、彼が来るのを

くび　　なが　　　　　　ま
首を長くして待っていた。

She was eagerly waiting for him to come back.

VOCABULARY:

彼女 *kanojo*—she
彼 *kare*—he
来る *kuru*—to come
待っていた *matteita*—was waiting

Idiom 71

たま
玉にきず

A fly in the ointment; a tiny flaw

- One small thing that ruins everything.
- Literally, "a scratch on a gem." For something as valuable and rare as a beautiful gem, even a tiny scratch can ruin it.

EXAMPLE SENTENCE:

かのじょ
彼女は、とてもきれいでやさしいが、

たま
おこりっぽいのが玉にきずだ。

She is very beautiful and nice, but her one flaw is her short temper.

VOCABULARY:

彼女 *kanojo*—she
とても *totemo*—very
きれい *kirei*—beautiful
やさしい *yasashii*—nice; kind
おこりっぽい *okorippoi*—tends to easily be angered

Idiom 72

のどから手が出る

て　で

Extremely tempting; mouthwatering

🛈 A common construction is 「のどから手が出るほど～がほしい。」 *nodo kara te ga deru hodo ~ ga hoshii.* I want ~ so bad.

🛈 Literally, "hand comes out of a mouth."

EXAMPLE SENTENCE:

借金で困っている彼にとって、

しゃっきん　　こま　　　　　　　　かれ

そのお金はのどから手が出るほどほ

かね　　　　　　　　　　て　で

しいものだった。

Being in such debt, that money was certainly tempting for him.

VOCABULARY:

借金 *shakkin*—debt
困っている *komatteiru*—troubled by (debt)
彼にとって kare *ni totte*—considering (the debt) he (owes)
その *sono*—that
お金 *okane*—money
ほど *hodo*—to such a degree
ほしいもの *hoshii mono*—something (he) wants

Idiom 73

ひとめ ひ
人目を引く

Eye-catching; conspicuous; noticeable

- This is mostly used with appearances such as flashy fashions or unusual hairstyles. It can also be used with loud voices in public areas.
- Literally, "pulls people's eyes." To pull people's eyes is to attract attention.

EXAMPLE SENTENCE:

かのじょ　　　　　　　　は　で　　ふく
彼女はいつも派手な服を

ひとめ　　ひ
きているので、人目を引く。

She always attracts attention with her flashy clothing.

VOCABULARY:

彼女 *kanojo*—she
いつも *itsumo*—always
派手 *hade*—flashy
服 *fuku*—clothes
きている *kiteiru*—wearing (clothes)
ので *node*—therefore; because

Idiom 74

み
身につく

Become accustomed (to a lifestyle...); master (a skill); become second nature

- When customs or techniques become second nature. Able to do something without thinking hard about it.
- Literally, "attach to oneself." Since this means something becomes a part of oneself, one can do it (use it) without thought.

EXAMPLE SENTENCE:

さいとう
斉藤さんは、きちんとした

み
マナーが身についている。

Saito is accustomed to proper manners.

VOCABULARY:

斉藤 *saitō*—Saito (name)

きちんと *kichinto*—properly; exactly

マナー *mana-*—manners

Idiom 75

おも　つぼ
思う壺

One's wishes; just as expected/wanted

- This is often used when something happens as planned.
- Literally, "the dice cup (the dice) one had in mind." The "*tsubo*" was originally from the dice cup used to shake dice while gambling. A talented dealer can shake the dice cup so the number he has in mind would appear.

EXAMPLE SENTENCE:

いま　　はんろん　　　　　　あいて　おも　つぼ
今、反論したら、相手の思う壺だ。

If you were to make your reply now, you'd be playing right into his hands.

VOCABULARY:

今 *ima*—now
反論 *hanron*—counterargument; a refutation
したら *shitara*—if you (make a counterargument)
相手 *aite*—opponent

Idiom 76

熱をあげる
ねつ

Become nuts over...; be mad about; be infatuated
with (a girl); lose one's head

- Use this with love crushes, hobbies, or things one loves in general.
- Literally, "to raise a fever."

EXAMPLE SENTENCE:

あの人は、有名な
ひと　　　　　　　ゆうめい

俳優に熱をあげている。
はいゆう　　ねつ

She's crazy about a famous performer.

VOCABULARY:

あの人 ano *hito*—that person
有名 *yuumei*—famous
俳優 *haiyuu*—performer; actor

Idiom 77

な
さじを投げる

To abandon hope; throw in the towel

- This can be used in any hopeless situation.
- Literally, "Throw away the spoon." The spoon here is used to mix medicine. If the doctor sees no hope (with medicine) in helping the patient, he throws the spoon away in despair.

EXAMPLE SENTENCE:

かれ　　　 いしゃ　　　　　　　　な
彼は、医者がさじを投げた

なんびょう　　　こくふく
難病を克服した。

He overcame a serious illness after the doctors threw in the towel.

VOCABULARY:

彼 *kare*—he
医者 *isha*—doctor
難病 *nanbyou*—serious illness
克服 *kokufuku*—overcome; bring under control

Idiom 78

穴があったら入りたい
あな　　　　　　はい

To be so ashamed one wishes to crawl in a hole

- Can be used whenever someone is extremely embarrassed.
- Literally, "If there were a hole, I'd like to enter." Also see 顔から火が出る *kao kara hi ga deru.* Burn with shame; be embarrassed.

EXAMPLE SENTENCE:

ズボンのおしりが破けていたなんて
知らなかった。穴があったら入りたい。

I didn't know my pants had a hole in the back; I feel so ashamed.

VOCABULARY:

ズボン *zubon*—pants
おしり *oshiri*—butt; backend
破けていた *yabuketeita*—was torn
なんて *nante*—such as (things such as holes in pants)
知らなかった *shiranakatta*—didn't know

Idiom 79

うわの空<ruby>空<rt>そら</rt></ruby>

Absent-mindedness; one's mind is elsewhere; inattentive

- Use this when someone should pay attention (such as in class, work, or when someone is speaking).
- They say this phrase has been used since the Heian Period (794 - 1185). This literally means, "the upper sky."

EXAMPLE SENTENCE:

君は授業中、うわの空で先生
の質問に答えられなかったね。

You were spaced out during class and couldn't answer the prof's question, weren't you?

VOCABULARY:

君 *kimi*—you
授業中 *jugyouchuu*—during class
先生 *sensei*—teacher
質問 *shitsumon*—question
答えられなかった *kotaerarenakatta*—couldn't answer
ね *ne*—weren't you?

Idiom 80

おおぶね　の　　　き　も
大船に乗った気持ち

To feel reassured; things will work out

- This is a metaphor for safety and a reliable foundation.
- Literally, "the feeling of boarding a large ship." Leaving a shaky, small boat in a rough sea for a large and stable ship is reassuring.

EXAMPLE SENTENCE:

わたし　　　　　もんだい　　かいけつ
私 がその問題を解決するから、

きみ　おおぶね　の　　　き　も　　　ま
君は大船に乗った気持ちで待ってい

なさい。

I'll find a solution to this problem; you just take it easy and wait.

VOCABULARY:

私 *watashi*—I
その *sono*—that
問題 *mondai*—problem
解決 *kaiketsu*—solve
から *kara*—because
君 *kimi*—you
待っていなさい *matteinasai*—wait
(command)

Idiom 81

かた　　かる
肩が軽くなる

Feel relieved; relieved of a responsibility

- Similar to the English expression, "That's a load off my shoulders."
- Literally, "shoulder becomes lighter." A similar Japanese expression is 「ほっとする。」

EXAMPLE SENTENCE:

もんだい　　かいけつ
やっとその問題が解決したので、

かた　　かる
肩が軽くなった。

I'll find a solution to this problem; you just take it easy and wait.

VOCABULARY:

やっと *yatto*—finally
その *sono*—that
問題 *mondai*—problem
解決 *kaiketsu*—solution
ので *node*—because

Idiom 82

き き
気が気でない

To feel uneasy; worry about; be beside oneself with worry

- Said when you can't relax or when worried.
- The 気 *ki* kanji has a multitude of meanings. This *ki* probably best means, "feeling" or "emotion." This phrase means, "one's current emotional state isn't normal."

EXAMPLE SENTENCE:

はじ　　　　ひ こ う き　　　の
初めて飛行機に乗った

き き
ときは、気が気でなかった。

The first time I rode on a plane, I was at my wit's end.

VOCABULARY:

初めて *hajimete*—first (time)
飛行機 *hikouki*—plane
乗った *notta*—rode
とき *toki*—time; the time

Idiom 83

き　お
気が置けない

To feel at home; easy to get along with; relaxed

- Another useful expression is *ki o tsukau* (lit. use care) which means "to fuss over" or "be overly concerned with someone's needs." This expression is the opposite; instead of "using thought or care," you don't have to mess with it at all.
- The "*ki*" here means "care" or "concern" (for one's proper place or manners). To not have to worry about (*okenai*) offending some social standard.

EXAMPLE SENTENCE:

き　お　　　　ともだち　おんせん　　　　　い
気が置けない友達と温泉にでも行きたい。

I'd like to go an onsen (public bath) with a friend with whom I can let down my hair.

VOCABULARY:

友達　*tomodachi*—friend
温泉　*onsen*—public bath
でも　*demo*—or the likes of (or something like onsen)
行きたい　*ikitai*—(I'd) like to go

Idiom 84

き　と
気を取られる

To be distracted by; be absorbed in...

- This is when one's thoughts are distracted by some outside source. For example, being distracted (absorbed) by conversation, you almost miss your train stop.
- The "*ki*" here means "thoughts" or "mind." The "*torareru*" means "to have taken away."

EXAMPLE SENTENCE:

き　と
テレビドラマに気を取られて、
りょうり　こ
料理を焦がしてしまった。

I was so absorbed by the TV drama, I burnt what I was cooking.

VOCABULARY:

テレビドラマ *terebi dorama*—TV drama
料理 *ryouri*—cooking
焦がしてしまった *kogashite shimatta*—
(unfortunately) burnt (the cooking)

Idiom 85

しっぽを出す
だ

To show one's true colors; give oneself away

- Said when one's secret is let out.
- Originated from legends of cunning foxes or raccoons in disguise. But when their tails stick out of the costume, their true form is known. A similar proverb is 頭隠して、尻隠さず *atama kakushite, shiri kakusazu.* Hide head, but didn't hide butt.

EXAMPLE SENTENCE:

はんにん
犯人は、とうとうしっぽを
だ　　　　けいさつ
出して警察につかまった。

The culprit at last gave himself away and the police caught him.

VOCABULARY:

犯人 *hannin*—culprit; criminal
とうとう *toutou*—at last; finally; in the end
警察 *keisatsu*—police
つかまった *tsukamatta*—caught (the criminal)

Idiom 86

て　　あし　　で
手も足も出ない

Can't do a thing; be at one's wit's end; be at a loss; helpless

- ❶ Use this phrase when there isn't the slightest chance for action—nothing can be done.
- ❶ Literally, "neither hands nor feet will go out." When no amount of hand (*te*) or foot (*ashi*) work will help a situation, you can say "neither hand nor foot sticks out."

EXAMPLE SENTENCE:

そのスパイは、自国の領事館に
逃げ込んだので、わが国の警察は手も
足もでない。

That spy took shelter in his own country's consulate so our country's police had their hands tied.

VOCABULARY:

その *sono*—that

スパイ *supai*—spy

自国 *jikoku*—(his) own country

領事館 *ryoujikan*—consulate

逃げ込んだ *nigekonda*—fled; ran away to...

ので *node*—therefore; because

わが国 *waga kuni*—my country

警察 *keisatsu*—police

Idiom 87

に　　　あし　　　ふ
二の足を踏む

Think twice; hesitate; second thoughts

- ❶ An idiom dictionary describes this as "hesitating after taking the first step."
- ❶ Literally, "to step with the second foot." The *"ni no ashi"* is probably only found in this expression.

EXAMPLE SENTENCE:

かれ
彼はスカイダイビングをしよう
おも　　　　　　　　　　　　たか　　　に　　　あし
と思ったが、あまりの高さに二の足を
ふ
踏んだ。

He wanted to go skydiving, but the extreme heights gave him second thoughts.

VOCABULARY:

彼 *kare*—he
スカイダイビング *sukaidaibingu*—skydiving
しようと思った *shiyou to omotta*—thought to
(go skydiving)
が *ga*—but
あまりの高さに *amari no takasa ni*—it was such a
height that...

Idiom 88

よろこ
ぬか喜び

Premature joy; crushed hopes

- This is used when a piece of good news turns out to be false.
- Literally, "rice-bran joy." The "*nuka*" is rice-bran—the pieces of husk and such separated after milling. But in recent times, 糠 *nuka* has come to mean something "small." From the "small" meaning, the meanings "fleeting" or "momentary" are derived. So the "joy" is "fleeting."

EXAMPLE SENTENCE:

やっと仕事が決まったと思ったのに、
その会社が倒産した。ぬか喜びだった。

I thought I had finally gotten a job but the company folded.
I got my hopes up.

VOCABULARY:

やっと *yatto*—finally; at last

仕事 *shigoto*—work

決まった *kimatta*—decided upon

と思った *to omotta*—thought

のに *noni*—although...

その *sono*—that

会社 *kasha*—company

倒産 *tousan*—bankrupt; go bust

Idiom 89

はな たか
鼻が高い

To be proud

- When someone is proud of some achievement.
- Literally, "tall nose." When someone is proud, they walk around with their nose high in the air.
- A secondary mean-ing is "to have a tall/big nose." Sometimes, Japanese will say foreigners have a "tall/big nose." This is a compliment since many Japanese believe their noses are too small.

EXAMPLE SENTENCE:

むすこ とうだい
息子が東大にはいったので、
とう はな たか
お父さんは鼻が高い。

The father was extremely proud of his son entering Tokyo University.

VOCABULARY:

息子 *musuko*—son
東大 *toudai*—Tokyo University (short for *tou-kyou daigaku*)
はいった *haitta*—entered
お父さん *otousan*—father

Idiom 90

はな
鼻にかける

To be proud; be boastful; brag

- Unlike "*hana ga takai*," this idiom has a more negative tone to it.
- Literally, "hanging on his nose"

EXAMPLE SENTENCE:

かのじょ　　　　　じぶん　　びじん　　　　　はな
彼女は、自分が美人だと鼻にかけている。

She was bragging about how beautiful she is.

VOCABULARY:

彼女 *kanojo*—she
自分 *jibun*—oneself
美人 *bijin*—a beautiful woman

Idiom 91

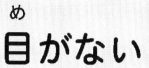

Extremely fond of; have a weakness or passion for...; be a sucker for...

- ❶ When one's love for something makes one blind to anything but that something, one loses all prudence and discretion.
- ❶ Literally, "no eyes (for anything but...)."

EXAMPLE SENTENCE:

私は、チョコレートに目がない。

I have a weakness for chocolate.

VOCABULARY:

私 *watashi*—I
チョコレート *chokore-to*—chocolate

Idiom 92

堂^{どう}に入^いる

To become an expert (at something); master something

- This usually implies years of careful practice (at some-thing), but it is often used to say a certain speech or performance was masterful.
- Literally, "to enter a temple." But the 堂 *dou* has taken on a meaning of "impressiveness" as in 堂々たる *doudoutaru* - stately; imposing; commanding; grand

EXAMPLE SENTENCE:

私^{わたし}の息子^{むすこ}のバイオリンの演奏^{えんそう}は、
堂^{どう}にいったものだった。

My son's violin performance was masterful.

VOCABULARY:

私の *watashi no*—my
息子 *musuko*—son
バイオリン *baiorin*—violin
演奏 *ensou*—(musical) performance

Idiom 93

あぶら　　　う

油を売る

To loaf; dawdle; dillydally; waste time (while one should be working)

- If someone should be doing work, but is chatting with his buddy about last night's game, he can be said to be "selling oil."
- In the Edo period (1603-1868), sellers of women's hair oil would strike up casual conversation and gossip in an effort to sell the oil.

EXAMPLE SENTENCE:

じかん　　　　　　　　　あぶら　う
こんな時間までどこで油を売っていたのか？

Where have you been loafing all this time?

VOCABULARY:

こんな *konna*—such as
時間 *jikan*—time
まで *made*—until (this time)
どこで *doko de*—where at

Idiom 94

うだつが上がらない
_あ

No hope for getting ahead; can't rise above mediocrity; can't get ahead

- When one's personal finances or environment don't improve.
- *"udatsu"* is a short pillar set on a beam to support the ridgepole. *"agaranai"* means "can't lift up." A house without *"udatsu"* cannot be raised.

EXAMPLE SENTENCE:

会社ではうだつが上がらない彼だが、
趣味の魚釣りでは一流だ。

He isn't able to get ahead at work, but as a hobby he is a first class fisherman.

VOCABULARY:

会社 *kaisha*—company
彼 *kare*—he
だが *da ga*—but
趣味 *shumi*—hobby
魚釣り *sakana tsuri*—fishing
一流 *ichiryuu*—first class

Idiom 95

かた　かぜ
肩で風をきる

To swagger; strut

- Use this idiom when you are on top of the world and your walk shows that.
- Literally, "to cut wind with shoulders."

EXAMPLE SENTENCE:

かいしゃ　　もう
会社が儲かっているので、

しゃちょう　かた　かぜ　き　　　ある
社長は肩で風を切って歩いている。

The company president went strutting about since the company had made a lot of money.

VOCABULARY:

会社 *kaisha*—company
儲かっている *moukatteiru*—making profit
ので *node*—therefore; because
社長 *shachou*—(company) president
歩いている *aruite iru*—walking

Idiom 96

けりをつける

To settle; finish off; close the book (on something)

- Said when ending something that is/has been difficult.
- This may have come from the use of "~*keri*" as an ender for classical poems.

EXAMPLE SENTENCE:

私は、この問題にもうけりをつけたいと思う。

I think I want to call it quits on this problem.

VOCABULARY:

私 *watashi*—I
この *kono*—this
問題 *mondai*—problem
もう *mou*—already; (not) any more
と思う *to omou*—(I) think

Idiom 97

なが　め　み
長い目で見る

To look at the long term

- Use this when thinking of the long run as opposed to seeing things in the short term.
- Literally, "look with a long eye."

EXAMPLE SENTENCE:

かいしゃ　かぶか　さ
この会社の株価は下がっているが、

なが　め　み
ぜひ長い目で見てほしい。きっと

しょうらい　　　　　　　おも
将来はあがると思う。

This company's stock is down, but please think of the long term. I'm sure it will go up in the future.

VOCABULARY:

この *kono*—this
会社 *kaisha*—company
株価 *kabuka*—price of a stock
下がっている *sagatteori*—dropping
ぜひ *zehi*—by all means
ほしい *hoshii*—want
きっと *kitto*—without fail; surely
将来 *shourai*—future
あがる *agaru*—rise
と思う *to omou*—(I) think; (I) believe

Idiom 98

ふで た
筆が立つ

A good writer; to write well

- ⓘ You can use this as a compliment to your penpal.
- ⓘ Literally, "the (writing) brush stands." The "*tatsu*" (stand) here means "skill." A similar example is 弁が立つ *ben ga tatsu* which means, "an eloquent speaker."

EXAMPLE SENTENCE:

こばやし　　　　　ふで　　た
小林さんは筆が立つので、

さっか　　　　　　　　　　おも
作家になればいいと思う。

Kobayashi is a great writer; I think she should become an author.

VOCABULARY:

小林 *kobayashi*—Kobayashi (name)
ので *node*—therefore; because
作家 *sakka*—writer
になればいい *ni nareba ii*—would be good to become (writer)
と思う *to omou*—(I) think; (I) believe

Idiom 99

ほね　　　お
骨が折れる

Something that requires a lot of effort; a hard job; no easy task

- This is often used with work: 骨が折れる仕事　*hone ga oreru shigoto* - "back breaking work." This is not used with fun activities.
- Literally, "bone breaks."

EXAMPLE SENTENCE:

とお　　　　い ど　　　　みず　く　　　　い
遠くの井戸まで水を汲みに行くのは、

ほね　お　　　　しごと
骨が折れる仕事だ。

Carrying water from a far well is back-breaking work.

VOCABULARY:

遠く *tooku*—far
井戸 *ido*—(water) well
まで *made*—until
水 *mizu*—water
汲みに行く *kumi ni iku*—to go and fetch
仕事 *shigoto*—work

Idiom 100

み　　　た
身を立てる

To make a success in life; rise in the world; make a living off of...

- This phrase can mean "to be a success" or "to make a living off of (doing something)."
- Literally, "stand someone up." This can be used to refer to oneself or others.

EXAMPLE SENTENCE:

わたし　　　はいゆう　　　　　　　　　　み
私は、俳優として身をたてることにした。

I decided to make a career as an actor.

VOCABULARY:

私 *watashi*—I
俳優 *haiyuu*—actor; actress
として *toshite*—as; in the capacity of...
こと *koto*—(makes a verb into a noun phrase)
にした *ni shita*—decided to...

Idiom 101

ねこ　　て　　　か
猫の手も借りたい

Very busy; short-handed; need help

- Whenever you are extremely busy, you would want even a "useless" animal like a cat to help out.
- Literally, "I'd like to borrow even a cat's hand." Since cats are not known for their productiveness, one would have to be extremely busy before even considering asking for the help of a cat.

EXAMPLE SENTENCE:

いま　　　　しゅうかく　　　いちばんいそが　　　　　じ　き
今は、収穫で一番忙しい時期な

　　　　　　　ねこ　て
ので、猫の手もかりたい。

Because the harvest right now is the busiest time of the year, I could use any-one's help.

VOCABULARY:

今 *ima*—now
収穫 *shuukaku*—harvest
一番 *ichiban*—#1; most; ~est
忙しい *isogashii*—busy
時期 *jiki*—time; season; time of the year
ので *node*—therefore

114

More by Clay & Yumi

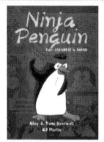

Ninja Penguin Talks Japanese in Japan
ISBN 978-1484825471

Hiragana, the Basics of Japanese
ISBN 978-1481863087

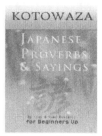

Kotowaza, Japanese Proverbs & Sayings
ISBN 978-1481904315

Japanese Reader Collection Vol 1
ISBN 978-1482373349

Japanese Reader Collection Vol 2
ISBN 978-1484191132

OTHER TITLES

Kanji 100: Learn the Most Useful Kanji in Japanese. ISBN 978-1482519815
Japanese Grammar 100 in Plain English. ISBN 978-1482536621

And: Katakana, Learn Japanese through Dialogues, Sound Words in Japanese, Haiku, Japanese Idioms, and others.

The Temporal
ISBN 978-1477406403

Fiction by CJ Martin

A Temporal Trust (Book two of The Temporal)
ISBN 978-1480119222

Two Tocks Before Midnight (An Agora Mystery)
eBook
The Penitent Thief (An Agora Mystery)
eBook

Tanaka and the Yakuza's Daughter
eBook

DOWNLOAD LINK

Download Link for the MP3s:

http://japanesereaders.com/1021

Thank you for purchasing and reading this book! To contact the authors, please email them at help@thejapanshop.com. See also the wide selection of materials for learning Japanese at www.TheJapanShop.com and the free site for learning Japanese www.thejapanesepage.com.

Made in the USA
San Bernardino, CA
08 September 2017